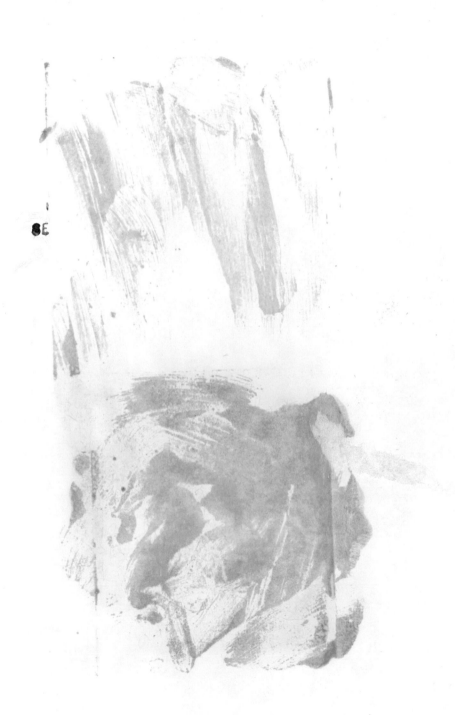

Everything You Need to Know About

BIRTH CONTROL

Birth control is the responsibility of both the man and woman.

• THE NEED TO KNOW LIBRARY •

Everything You Need to Know About

BIRTH CONTROL

Gary Mucciolo, M.D.

Series Editor: Evan Stark, Ph.D.

THE ROSEN PUBLISHING GROUP, INC.
NEW YORK

Published in 1990 by The Rosen Publishing Group, Inc.
29 East 21st Street, New York City, New York 10010

First Edition
Copyright 1990 by The Rosen Publishing Group, Inc.

Manufactured in the United States of America.

Library of Congress Cataloging-in-Publication Data

Mucciolo, Gary.
    Everything you need to know about birth control.
    (The Need to know library)
    Includes bibliographical references.
    Index.
    Summary: Discusses the reproductive system and the various methods of
birth control and how they work.
    ISBN 0-8239-1014-8
    1. Contraception—Juvenile literature. 2. Teenage
pregnancy—Prevention—Juvenile literature. [1. Birth
control. 2. Pregnancy. 3. Sexual ethics] I. Title.
II. Series.
RG136.3.M83   1989
613.9′4   89-70104
                                                                  CIP
                                                                   AC

Contents

Introduction

Why Birth Control Is Important

Teens often use sex to try to gain status. Teens often feel pressure to have sex and to talk about their sexual experiences. Those who choose not to have sex feel "out of it." The teens who are "doing it" are often considered "cool" and grown-up. But those teens who get *pregnant* are not thought of as very cool by anyone.

Some teens feel that having a baby is a sign of being grown-up. Many young women feel that having a baby will make everyone see them as an adult. Many young men think that fathering a baby shows the world that they are manly. But often the opposite is true. Most teens with babies show the world just how young they really are. And they show the world that they are not yet ready to handle the responsibilities of being parents.

One cause of teen pregnancy is not having the facts. There are many "myths" about birth control. Those are things that people think are true but are not. If you don't know about them, you can easily become pregnant by accident:

○ You CAN get pregnant even if you have sex standing up.
○ You CAN get pregnant while you have your period.
○ You CAN get pregnant after an abortion.
○ You CAN get pregnant even if the man doesn't have an orgasm in the vagina.
○ You CAN get pregnant even if you douche after sex.
○ You CAN get pregnant if you use contraceptive foam after sex.
○ You CAN get pregnant even if you are breast-feeding.

So what is the best thing to do? The best thing is to learn how to have sex *responsibly*. And to remember what you learned if you decide to have sex.

This book is about contraception. It is about sexual responsibility. Contraception is preventing pregnancy. It is using birth control.

Responsible sex is the job of *both* the man and the woman. Too many people think that birth control is the woman's responsibility. And too many people think that if a woman gets pregnant she was "not careful enough." But that is not true. It takes two people for a woman to become pregnant. Each of those people is equally responsible. Birth control is as much a man's responsibility as a woman's.

FEMALE REPRODUCTIVE SYSTEM

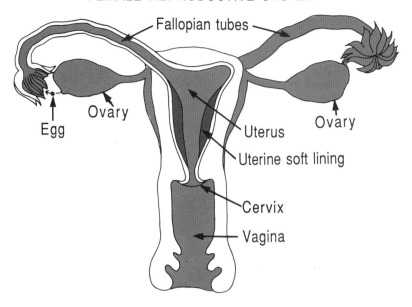

Fallopian tubes

Ovary

Egg

Ovary

Uterus

Uterine soft lining

Cervix

Vagina

MALE REPRODUCTIVE SYSTEM

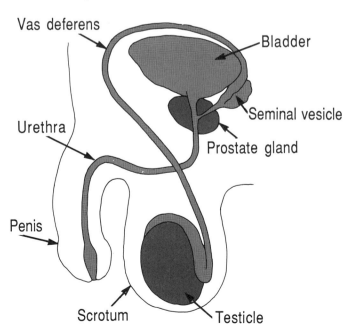

Vas deferens

Bladder

Seminal vesicle

Urethra

Prostate gland

Penis

Scrotum

Testicle

Chapter 1

The Male and The Female Body

To prevent pregnancy you have to know how the human body works. It helps to understand how pregnancy happens.

The Male Body

Males fertilize female eggs with sperm. Sperm is produced by males in their testicles (*balls*). The sperm, in a liquid, is released during sex. It is placed by the penis into the woman's vagina. If a sperm reaches the egg in the woman's body, it fertilizes the egg. The woman becomes pregnant.

Sperm lives best in a temperature lower than 98.6 degrees Fahrenheit (the temperature inside the body). The testicles are in a sac outside the body. This keeps the sperm a little cooler.

When he is sexually excited, a male's penis becomes hard. This is called an erection. When he is completely stimulated, the male has an orgasm (he ejaculates, or comes). A whitish liquid is released. It contains sperm and fluids from other glands. The liquid is released from the penis in spurts during orgasm. The average ejaculation contains up to 500 million sperm and would fill half a teaspoon. But only *one* of those 500 million sperm is needed to fertilize an egg.

The Female Body

Most of the female sex organs are inside the body. What can be seen is pubic hair and the labia (lips) that cover the opening of the vagina. The labia start at the *clitoris*. The clitoris is a small bump under the pubic bone. It is filled with sensitive nerves that become excited and enlarged during sex. When the clitoris becomes fully excited, a woman has an orgasm. During orgasm a woman has muscle contractions much like a man's. A woman also may release some liquid during orgasm.

At the opening of the vagina is a piece of tough skin. This skin is called a *hymen*. The hymen tears during a woman's first sexual intercourse. There is often some bleeding when the hymen breaks. The first time is usually a little uncomfortable. But the hymen heals very rapidly. So sex is not uncomfortable in the future.

The walls of the vagina are lined with mucous membranes. The mucous membranes are wet, soft tissue, like those inside the mouth. There is no space in the vagina. It is like a collapsed tube. The vaginal walls expand during sex to have enough room for the penis. The walls separate when a penis is inserted.

The cervix is the opening to the *uterus* (womb). It is at the top of the vagina. Sperm travel through the cervix to reach the uterus. Then they travel to the fallopian tubes. These are attached to the uterus on the left and right. They lead from the uterus to the ovaries, where the eggs are stored.

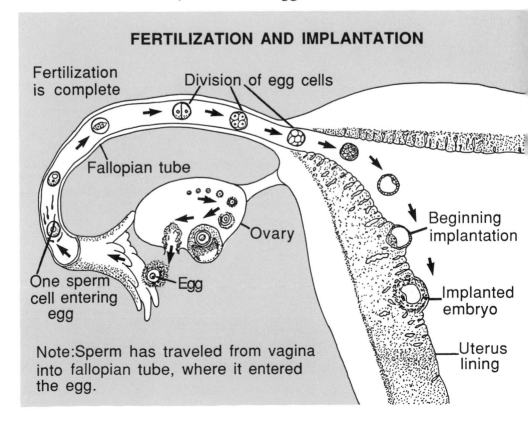

FERTILIZATION AND IMPLANTATION

Fertilization is complete

Division of egg cells

Fallopian tube

Ovary

One sperm cell entering egg

Egg

Beginning implantation

Implanted embryo

Uterus lining

Note:Sperm has traveled from vagina into fallopian tube, where it entered the egg.

The complete menstrual cycle takes about twenty-eight days.

Chapter 2

The Menstrual Cycle and Fertility

The bleeding a woman experiences each month is called her menstrual period. It is also called "my friend," or "the curse." This comes at the end of the woman's menstrual cycle. The entire cycle takes about 28 days. The closer a woman gets to the middle of her cycle, the more fertile she will be. The middle of the cycle is ovulation. Ovulation is when an egg is released into a fallopian tube. During ovulation a woman's fertility is at its peak.

Each month the female body gets ready to be pregnant. The walls of the uterus become thick in order to protect a fetus. When the body knows it is not pregnant that month, it gets rid of the thickened lining of the uterus. The lining falls off the wall of the uterus and travels down through the cervix. From the cervix it flows out of the vagina. That is when a woman has a menstrual period.

Most women have their first period between the ages of 9 and 15. The average age in the United States is 12. The average time between periods is about 28 days. Bleeding is different in every woman. On the average a woman bleeds for 3 to 7 days. The heaviest bleeding is usually on the first two days.

Menopause is when the cycle stops. Menopause occurs in late middle age. The average age for menopause in the United States is 51. When a woman stops having her periods, certain hormones in her body are reduced. It also means she can no longer become pregnant.

Fertility

Fertility is related to the menstrual cycle. It is important to know what happens at each stage.

During the first few days of the cycle (right after bleeding stops) the ovaries produce estrogen. Estrogen is a female hormone. The estrogen stimulates about six eggs in the ovaries. But only one egg will grow large enough to survive. The others will stop growing and will dissolve.

By the end of the second week, the egg is ready. It will be released into a fallopian tube. Before it is released, a pool of fluid grows around it. The fluid is called a cyst or follicle. The cyst then breaks open and releases the egg. The release of the egg is called ovulation. The egg is released into a fallopian tube, where it may be fertilized. The egg travels down the fallopian tube to the uterus.

Once the egg is released, it must be fertilized within 24 hours. If it is not fertilized, it dissolves. Sperm can live up to three days inside the female body. *A woman can become pregnant if she has unprotected sex three days before she ovulates.*

The days right before and during ovulation are the most "fertile" days. That means the chances for pregnancy are greatest during these days. But that does not mean a woman cannot get pregnant during the other days of the month. One thing is very important to remember. It is possible for a woman to become pregnant *at any time during the month.* Changes in the ovulation cycle can occur every month. Monthly changes in bleeding are also common. These kinds of changes make "fertile days" hard to know. Many women have some bleeding during the month. These women often think that the bleeding is their period. Sometimes it is not. Many women mistake vaginal bleeding or vaginal discharge for their period. Then they have sex, thinking that they are safe. They can become pregnant this way. Unprotected sex is very risky *at any time of the month.*

During puberty many bodily changes occur.

Chapter 3

Adolescence and The Changing Body

Adolescence and puberty (pyoo-ber-tee) are times of great change. They also can be times of fear and worry. Adolescence is the teen years, the time between puberty and maturity. Puberty is the time when the body changes from a child's body to that of an adult. Most people start puberty between the ages of 9 and 14.

Many of the body's changes during puberty involve the sexual and reproductive organs. Most changes are caused by an increase in hormones. Hormones are a group of the body's chemicals.

The changing body begins to look different. For a man, puberty means the growth of pubic hair, facial hair, and growth in the size of the penis and testicles. For a woman, puberty means the growth of pubic hair and the growth of breasts.

In addition to all these physical changes, teens must deal with emotional changes, too. With the growth of the genitals and hormones, teens begin to think about sex. There are social pressures. Teens become very aware of how they look. And they often feel very awkward about themselves.

Male Puberty and Fertility

Usually the first sign of puberty for young men is pubic hair growth. Then the testicles and penis grow larger. Often this is joined by a cracking voice. Armpit hair begins to grow. Some boys have a growth spurt in height. Many boys then get acne or pimples. When the acne begins to go away, many boys begin to grow facial hair.

A young man in puberty will probably have what are called "wet dreams." He dreams, usually about sex, and then his body releases sperm. This is called ejaculation (ee-jack-yoo-lay-shun). It usually happens while asleep. Most young men have their first wet dream about a year after their first signs of puberty. This is usually about age thirteen.

As a young man gets older, his sperm becomes more powerful. By the time young men have facial hair, they are fully fertile. But this does not mean young men should not use birth control. It does NOT mean that men without facial hair cannot father children. Any man who can get an erection and ejaculate (release sperm) can become a father.

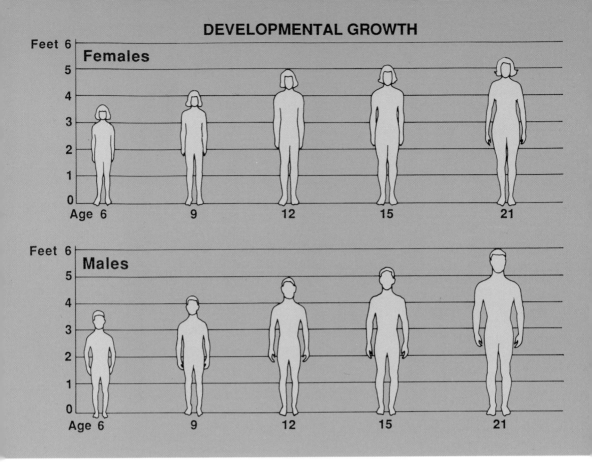

DEVELOPMENTAL GROWTH

Females

Feet 6, 5, 4, 3, 2, 1, 0

Age 6, 9, 12, 15, 21

Males

Feet 6, 5, 4, 3, 2, 1, 0

Age 6, 9, 12, 15, 21

Female Puberty and Fertility

Females usually have their first period around age twelve. But this is not the first sign of puberty. In fact, it is one of the last. The first sign of puberty is breast budding. This is not the growth of full breast development. It is the growth of a small round mound under the nipple. The next sign that appears is pubic hair. Then hair begins to grow in the armpits. The last sign is menstrual bleeding.

A young woman's first period is not the first time she can get pregnant. It is possible for a woman to become pregnant *before* her first period.

A gynecologist (guy-neh-cah-low-jist) is a doctor who takes medical care of women. There are two reasons for a young woman to see a gynecologist. One reason is if her first period has not come by the time she is sixteen. The other reason is if she is thinking about becoming sexually active. The doctor can give excellent birth control advice.

A gynecologist will also do important check ups each year. The doctor will examine the vagina, the cervix, the ovaries, and the uterus. She or he will check to make sure a sexually active patient's body remains healthy. Tests for sexually transmitted diseases (STDs) can also be done.

A gynecologist can also do another test. This test is called a "pap smear." A pap smear checks the condition of the cervix. First the doctor touches the tip of the cervix with a Q-tip. Then a tiny bit of tissue is gently scraped from the area. This does not hurt. The test takes only about two minutes. This test will detect any hint of cancer of the cervix. Cervical cancer is very rare. But if it is untreated, it can be very serious. A pap test can also show signs of some STDs. *Herpes* and *chlamydia* can be detected with a pap smear.

Most gynecologists take privacy very seriously. They will not tell about your sex life to anyone, including your parents. All patients are treated as adults. And their privacy must be respected. Any doctor who does not give this kind of care is not practicing well.

Chapter 4

Some Facts About Birth Control

There are many different kinds of birth control methods available today. You should ask two things about each product. The first is how well does it work? The second thing to think about is how safe is it to use? Some birth control products are more effective and safe than others. Each product is used differently. If a contraceptive (birth control product) is not used in the right way, it will not work to prevent pregnancy. In the following chapters we will talk about the most popular methods of contraception. And we will explain how to use each one so it will work well.

Use of each method needs planning. Some can be used hours before sex. Others must be used right before sex. None should be used AFTER sex. Many young people think birth control is a "pain." They feel it is not easy to use. And they feel it "spoils the moment." They don't want to think about birth control during sex.

Many contraceptives take only a minute or two to use. This minute provides very important protection. That is why planning ahead of time is a good idea.

IMPORTANT INFORMATION ABOUT DOUCHING

Some young people use douches (dooshes) because they think that will give protection from pregnancy. Nothing you do AFTER sex will protect you very well. Douching is used to clean the vagina. Young women often use a douche after having sex. Some women use a vinegar solution. Others use douches you can buy in a drugstore. Those are safe, but they should not be used for birth control. Some teens use a method of douching that is useless and also *dangerous*. They shake up a bottle of cola and release the liquid into the vagina. This will *not* prevent pregnancy. Cola does not kill sperm. And pressure may force the sperm further up into the vagina. Even worse, the cola can cause an infection. Or a woman can have an allergic reaction. Never force any substance under pressure into the vagina.

What's on the Market

All available contraceptives are safe to use. Some have side effects if you use them for a long time. A side effect is another effect of a medication on your body. We will discuss those one at a time. The use of some contraceptives is riskier for some people than for others. We will talk about those things too.

Not every kind of birth control is right for everyone. That is why you should speak with a doctor before you have sex. A doctor can help you figure out which methods are best for you.

Some products must be fitted or prescribed by a doctor. A prescription is a note from the doctor telling the druggist what to give you. A diaphragm or a cervical cap must be fitted by a doctor. That will make sure that it works properly. And a doctor can prescribe a birth control pill for you. Or he will tell you why you should not use it.

Things to Keep in Mind

1. Each birth control method has some possible risk to health. But these risks are very small. And very rare. The products are very safe. They are approved for everyday use all over the world.
2. No method or product is 100 percent failure-proof. But many products are very reliable. With regular, proper use the chances of becoming pregnant are very small.
3. Some birth control methods have extra benefits. Some help to prevent sexually transmitted diseases. The condom, for example, greatly reduces the chances of spreading the AIDS virus. Other contraceptives reduce the risks of certain types of cancer.
4. There is only one 100 percent sure way to avoid pregnancy: do not have sex.

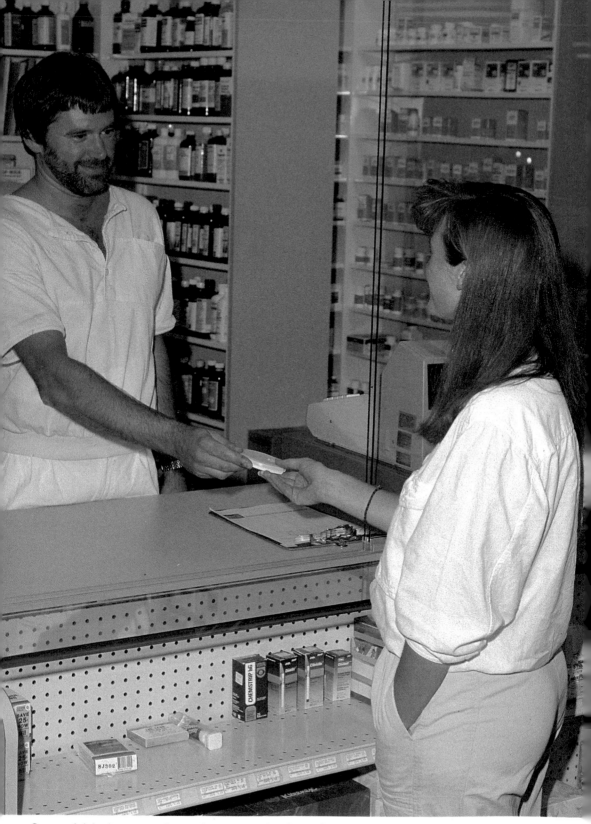

Several birth control products can be bought without a prescription.

Chapter 5

Abstinence, Rhythm, Withdrawal

Every person has a different pattern of sexual behavior. Some people have sex often. Others have sex only once in a while. Others do not have sex at all. Your sexual pattern will help you decide which method of birth control is best for you.

Abstinence (Not Having Sex)

Effectiveness:	HIGHEST POSSIBLE
Health Safety:	Very High
How It Works:	No sex, no chance of pregnancy
Side Effects:	None
Side Benefits:	No chance of sexually transmitted disease
What People Falsely Think:	Pent-up sexual energy will cause problems

Abstinence means not having sex at all. Abstinence is the only 100 percent guaranteed way to make sure you or your partner don't get pregnant. Abstinence does not mean no kissing or hugging. It doesn't even mean no "petting." It just means no genital-to-genital contact. That means the penis does not enter or go near the vagina.

Whenever a penis releases sperm in or near the vagina you can get pregnant. Many people think that if the penis doesn't enter the vagina you can't get pregnant. But that is not completely true.

If sperm gets on the leg or thigh it can get into the vagina. Or sperm can get on the fingers of the man or woman. Then the fingers with sperm can touch or enter the vagina. This can be risky, though chances of pregnancy are very low.

Abstinence has another benefit. It means you will not get a sexually transmitted disease (STD).

Some people believe that young males will be damaged by not releasing sexual energy. That is not true. Young men and women may feel an intense desire for physical contact. But there is no harm in not having sex. There are also no dangers from masturbation (self-stimulation).

Men and women, married and single, young and old, masturbate. It is perfectly healthy and safe.

Many teens today feel pressured to have sex. Teens often think that sex makes them "mature." But there has been a shift in the way teens think about sex. More teens are thinking about more careful sex. And more teens are thinking about monogamy (having one serious relationship and no others). Marriage is even becoming popular again.

There should never be pressure on teens to have sex. Sex is a very personal thing. The choice to have sex is very private.

An unwanted pregnancy can cause many problems.

There is nothing wrong with being a virgin. And there is nothing wrong with waiting until you are older or married to have sex. That is true for both men and women. When to have sex is your own personal choice. No one has the right to judge your decision.

Rhythm (Sometime Abstinence)

Effectiveness:	POOR
Health Safety:	High
How It Works:	Attempt to have sex before or after ovulation
Side Effects:	None
Side Benefits:	Natural form of birth control
What People Falsely Think:	Having sex only during ovulation results in pregnancy

Sometime abstinence means sometimes not having sex. Having sex well before or well after ovulation is less likely to result in pregnancy. Sometime abstinence is also called the "rhythm method" of birth control. That is because sex is planned according to the rhythm of ovulation. Ovulation is the monthly release of the egg.

The rhythm method is considered "natural family planning." It is the only method approved by the Catholic Church for married couples. However, using the rhythm method is complicated. And it has poor results. It is a very poor method for teens.

Having sex before or after ovulation only *reduces* the chances of becoming pregnant. It *does not* mean that sex will not result in pregnancy. A *woman can become pregnant at any time during the month.* She can get pregnant even while she has her period. Ovulation can be irregular. And bleeding can result from something other than a normal period.

The rhythm method depends on knowing when ovulation occurs. But ovulation is hard to figure out. It doesn't always happen at the same time every month. So you have to chart the dates of your period for a long time. And you must keep track of other signs during the month. These other signs include body temperature and the thickness of mucus in the cervix. This charting helps you find your ovulation and fertility patterns. But even the best charting results are not very good. All in all, this is a highly unreliable method of birth control. It is *not* recommended for teens.

Withdrawal

Effectiveness:	VERY POOR
Health Safety:	High
How It Works:	The penis is pulled out before ejaculation
Side Effects:	None
Side Benefits:	None
What People Falsely Think:	There is no chance of pregnancy if the penis is not in the vagina during orgasm

Withdrawal is one of the birth control methods teens use the most. Unfortunately, it is a very poor one. This popular method was practiced by many teens who are now parents. There are a few reasons why this method doesn't work very well. The erect penis often leaks sperm. The penis in the vagina can leak sperm even without an orgasm. Sperm can travel up through the uterus and cause pregnancy. It is often hard for a man to stop himself in the middle of sex. Most men cannot pull out of the vagina when they are highly excited. The result is orgasm in the vagina. That is the very thing the man is trying not to do. Many men cannot tell when they are about to ejaculate. It happens suddenly. They have no warning in time to pull out. The results can be a disaster. A pregnancy can occur.

Friends can share good advice about birth control.

Chapter 6

The Pill

SCENE:	The high school cafeteria.
JEAN:	I'm afraid, Maria. I think I might be pregnant.
MARIA:	Why do you think that?
JEAN:	Well . . . Tommy and I had sex the other night. And we didn't use any protection.
MARIA:	He didn't have a condom?
JEAN:	No. He said he ran out and forgot to buy some more.
MARIA:	But you had sex anyway?
JEAN:	Well, we got started. And then, right in the middle, he tells me he doesn't have anything. It's kind of hard to stop then.
MARIA:	Yeah. I know.
JEAN:	I just hate finding out in the middle that we don't have any protection. And we end up doing it anyway.
MARIA:	It sounds to me like you should start taking the pill instead. That might solve your problems.
JEAN:	Really? Where do I get it?
MARIA:	You have to get a prescription from your doctor.

The Pill

Effectiveness:	VERY HIGH
Health Safety:	Medium to High
How It Works:	Taken orally every day
Side Effects:	Possible weight gain, nausea, depression, irregular menstruation
Side Benefits:	Reduces menstrual cramps, helps to prevent ovarian cysts, reduces menstrual blood loss and protects against anemia, reduces chances of pelvic infections, helps protect against uterine and ovarian cancer, eliminates ovulation discomfort
OTHER FACTS:	It is not dangerous. It does not cause cancer.

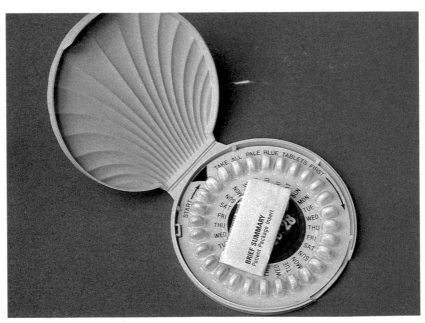

The "Pill" must be taken every day in order to give full protection.

Birth control medication is known commonly as "the pill." It is very reliable. And it is very easy to use. You take the pill once a day. The only important thing to remember is that *it must be taken every day*. The pill will not work properly unless you use it every day. It must become a daily routine, like brushing your teeth.

The pill is also quite easy to get. All you need is a prescription from your doctor.

Many people like using the pill. You do not have to interrupt sex to be protected. As long as a woman takes the pill every day, she does not have to plan birth control before sex. Neither the man nor the woman needs to stop in the middle of sex. This way, sex can be completely spontaneous (on the spur of the moment). And you are never "caught" at an awkward moment without protection.

How the Pill Works

The pill is made from two hormones (chemicals). They are like the hormones a woman's body produces. The hormones fool the body into thinking it is pregnant. As a result, the ovaries do not release new eggs in the middle of each monthly cycle. And without the release of eggs, there is practically no chance of pregnancy.

How to Take the Pill

The pill is taken by mouth every day. The pills come in packages that have enough pills for a whole month. It is important to follow the instructions on the package. Sometimes certain pills must be taken on certain days. The labeling on the package explains the way to take them.

Forgetting to Take the Pill

The pill does not work if it is not taken according to the schedule. If one day is missed, the user's chances of pregnancy become greater for the rest of that month. There are some ways to reduce the risks if a pill is missed. If one pill is missed, take two pills the next day as soon as you remember. Then go back to the normal schedule. If two pills are missed, two pills should be taken as soon as you remember. Then another two pills should be taken the next day. Then go back to the normal schedule. This method is only to help reduce the chances of pregnancy. It is not sure to be effective. If you miss a pill, it is best to double up AND to use an additional method of birth control until the new cycle begins. You should finish the month's supply of pills on schedule. But you should also use another form of contraception (diaphragm, condom, etc.) whenever you have sex. Then, after the end of the cycle, start a new package of pills.

Stopping the Pill

Stopping the pill is easy. You just stop taking it. It may take a little while for your periods to come back on a normal cycle.

Doctors tell women to be off the pill for two to three months before trying to get pregnant. But there are no dangers if you stop the pill and become pregnant right away.

Side Effects

There are usually a few side effects with the pill. The side effects can include weight gain, breast tenderness, bloating, and irregular bleeding. The pill can also cause nausea (feeling that you want to throw up). The weight gain usually lasts for only a little while. Lowering calories just a little bit and exercising can help avoid gaining weight. The nausea will also go away. Usually it is gone completely by the third month you take the pills. It is always better to take the pill on a full stomach or just before bed.

A very small number of women get depressed when they take the pill. Some women experience irregular bleeding when they are on the pill. Sometimes this means they menstruate in mid-cycle. Other times their period does not come at all. This can be dangerous, because a missed period can be the first sign of pregnancy. If you miss a period when you are taking the pill, you should see a doctor.

Health Risks

The risk to health from the pill is very small. Doctors advise women not to smoke while on the pill. Taking the pill and smoking can increase the chances of a stroke. A rare but important danger is the tendency of some women on the pill to develop blood clots. A tiny barrier can form in the veins or arteries. The barrier prevents blood from flowing. The blood clot can cause heart attacks or strokes. The pill can also cause temporary high blood pressure in some women. But the cases of these risks are very few, and very rare.

Getting the Pill

The pill cannot be bought over the counter. You must have a prescription from a doctor. A month's supply of pills will cost about fifteen dollars. Many clinics provide discounted or free pills for teens.

Other Oral Contraception

Teens may know about the "morning-after" pill. This is a pill that will stop pregnancy if it has occurred. It is usually given only to women who have been raped. Occasionally a teen will be able to get one from her doctor. But it is up to the doctor. The morning-after pill is not 100 percent guaranteed and can be dangerous. It is not really a form of "birth control." It does not prevent conception. It only stops it afterward.

Chapter 7

The Condom

SCENE: Randy's car.

RANDY: Come on , Teresa, let's do it here. It's
           quiet and no one's around.

TERESA: I didn't bring my birth control with
           me.

RANDY: What? Why not?

TERESA: I thought it was here in my bag but it
           isn't. I put it in my other bag by
           mistake.

RANDY: Oh, great. That's just great. How could
           you do something like that?

TERESA: It was a mistake.

RANDY: A mistake. You should think about
           these things. It's your responsibility.

TERESA: You should think about it too. Why is
           it only my responsibility?

RANDY: Because you're the one that's gonna get
           pregnant.

TERESA: Well, if I get pregnant, that concerns you as much as me.

RANDY: But it's not the same. Birth control is the woman's responsibility.

TERESA: I won't accept that at all. It's as much your responsibility as it is mine. From now on, YOU are responsible for our birth control.

RANDY: Aw, Teresa, come on.

TERESA: We'll have sex when we have protection. I'm not carrying my stuff around anymore. At least not for a while.

RANDY: But why?

TERESA: Because you need to realize that birth control is a man's responsibility too.

The Condom

Effectiveness:	HIGH
Health Safety:	Very High
How It Works:	A rubber sheath is placed over the erect penis before sex
Side Effects:	None
Side Benefits	Greatly reduces the chances of contracting many sexually transmitted diseases
OTHER FACTS:	Never use the same condom twice. One size fits all.

A condom is a rubber shield that fits over the erect penis before sex. A condom prevents the sperm from entering the vagina. Condoms are also known as "rubbers," "prophylactics," and "safes." They are a very effective method of contraception. Condoms are also cheap and easy to use.

Many clinics and campus health centers give out condoms free. They are widely available and easy to find. That is why there is no excuse not to use them.

A few things about condoms are different from other birth control methods. First, condoms are the only common form of birth control that is used by the man. With condom use, birth control is the man's responsibility. Second, condoms are the only form of birth control that gives good protection against sexually transmitted diseases (STDs). They form a shield between the partners' genitals. That means that bodily fluids are not exchanged. And that means the chances of transmitting or getting an STD are greatly reduced. Using condoms is part of "safer sex." And "safer sex" is smart sex.

How to Use a Condom

Condoms can be bought in most drugstores. You can now buy them in many other stores as well. Condoms come in one size. They are made of an elastic material that stretches to fit any size penis. Putting on the condom is simple. You roll it up over the erect penis before sex. It is important to

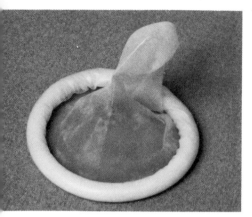

put the condom on as soon as the penis is erect. That is because sperm can slip out of the erect penis before sex. So it is safest to have the penis covered as soon as it is erect.

When you put on the condom, be careful. If a condom is pulled on too tight, it may rip or tear. That would make the condom useless. It is good to hold the tip closed when you put on a condom. That helps to leave a space at the end to collect the sperm. The condom-covered penis should not stay inside the vagina after orgasm. That is because the penis gets soft soon after orgasm. And when the penis gets soft, the condom can slip off easily. Sperm can spill into the vagina. That would ruin the condom's effectiveness.

Never use the same condom more than once. And used condoms should be disposed of properly. Do not try to flush condoms down the toilet.

Things to Remember

You must use a condom each time you have sex. And you can never re-use a condom.

Some condoms are coated with a spermicide (sperm-killing substance). That makes them even more effective as birth control. The cost of condoms is quite low. A box of a dozen costs around $9.00.

Chapter 8

The Diaphragm and the Cervical Cap

SCENE: The gynecologist's office.

DR. WATSON: What can I do for you today, Wendy?

WENDY: Well, I'd like to be fitted for a diaphragm.

DR. WATSON: Very well. Why now?

WENDY: Well, I have just started to be sexually active. And I would like to have a method of birth control that I can carry with me in my purse. Or that I can wear. I heard a diaphragm was a good choice.

DR. WATSON: Yes, it is. And I can fit you with one and show you how to put it in. It's quite easy.

WENDY: Is it true that I can put it in a while before sex? So I don't have to think about it during sex?

DR. WATSON: Yes. But it is best not to put it in more than an hour ahead of time.

WENDY: I see. Good.

The Diaphragm

Effectiveness:	HIGH
Health Safety:	Very Good
How It Works:	A rubber dish is placed over the opening of the cervix to prevent sperm from traveling through to the uterus
Side Effects:	Can cause cramps and discomfort in some women
Side Benefits:	Can be inserted before sex so there is no interruption
What People Falsely Think:	It is hard to put in

A diaphragm (die-uh-fram) is a rubber cup (or dish) that is filled with spermicide and inserted into the vagina. In the vagina, it rests against the pubic bone and covers the opening to the cervix. The diaphragm will partly block the sperm from entering the uterus. The key is the spermicide. It will kill any sperm that have passed around the diaphragm.

Diaphragms come in many different sizes. That is because women have different size pubic bones and different size cervixes. Each woman must be fitted for a diaphragm. A doctor will give you the right size diaphragm for your body. And a doctor will show you how to put the diaphragm in and take it out. Some people think putting in a diaphragm is hard. But it only looks hard at first. After two or three practices, anyone can do it.

How to Use a Diaphragm

A diaphragm can be put in up to one hour before sex. Before it is put in, it is rubbed with a generous amount of spermicide or contraceptive jelly. The jelly or cream increases the diaphragm's effectiveness and makes it easier to insert. Then the diaphragm is pinched together with one hand. The other hand separates the lips of the vagina. The diaphragm is then inserted into the vagina as far as it will go. It should wind up resting over the cervix and against the pubic bone. It is easiest to do this in one of three positions: 1) lying on your back, knees up, 2) squatting, 3) standing, with one leg propped up.

It is easy to check the position of the diaphragm by inserting a finger into the vagina. The edge of the diaphragm should be up against the pubic bone. Checking this sounds more complicated than it is. Don't worry. Once a diaphragm is in, it is very hard for it to rest in any position that is not the right one. A little practice will help a lot too.

The diaphragm must stay in for six to eight hours after sex. Most women can walk around without any discomfort. They don't even feel the diaphragm.

The diaphragm can be removed easily. Place your fingers into the vagina. Then reach up and hook the rim with a finger. The diaphragm will slide out easily.

Maintaining Your Diaphragm

Remove the diaphragm and wash it with soap and water. Be sure to rinse it thoroughly. You do not want to leave soap on it. Dry the diaphragm completely and store it in its carrying case. A diaphragm can dry out and crack if it is left out in the air for too long.

It is important to wash and dry your diaphragm after each use and again before the next use. The only substances that should go on it are spermicides or jellies. Be sure the jelly you use is made for use with diaphragms. The jellies that are not meant for use with diaphragms can cause the rubber to come apart.

Always remember to check your diaphragm for holes. This can be done by holding it up to the light. If there are any holes or cracks, throw it out and get a new one. A diaphragm usually costs about $20. Spermicides and jellies cost about $9 to $14 per tube. But the tube will last for a while. There will also be a charge from your doctor for an office visit. But if the total is divided by the entire year, it is a relatively cheap method of birth control.

Benefits of a Diaphragm

Diaphragms have almost no health risks or side effects. When used with spermicides or jellies, they may reduce the spread of some STDs, but that is not certain.

Diaphragms can be inserted as long as an hour before sex. That way there is no interruption during sex.

Another benefit of the diaphragm is "cleaner" sex during menstruation. Many people do not want to have sex during

menstruation. The diaphragm stops the flow of blood. Sex will not be as messy during this time.

The Cervical Cap

The cervical cap is really just a smaller version of the diaphragm. It is a small rubber cap that is inserted into the vagina to cover the cervix. Because it is smaller, it can be worn longer than a diaphragm. But it is also harder to insert. And it is not clear exactly how long the cervical cap can be worn at any one time. Since the cervical cap does not have any clear advantages over the diaphragm, it is not as popular. And it is not as widely available in this country.

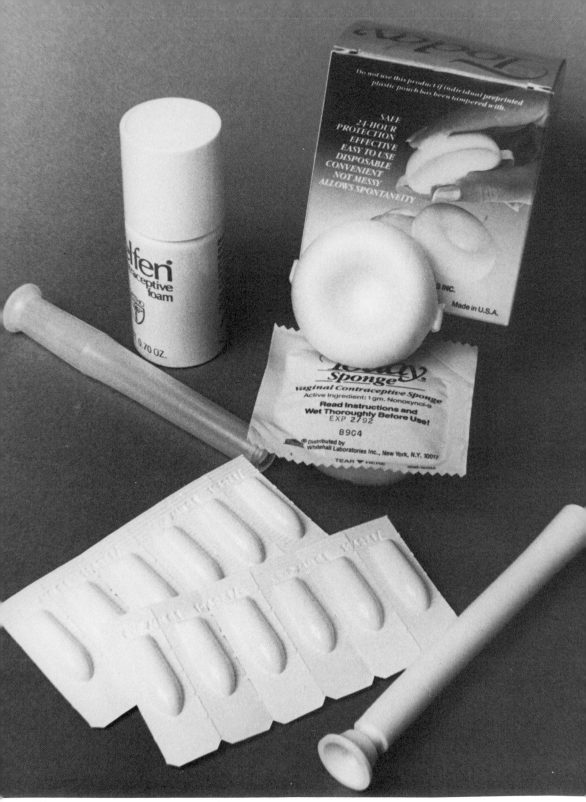

The sponge, contraceptive foams, and vaginal suppositories are available without prescription.

Chapter 9

The Sponge

SCENE: On the phone with Margie and Helena.

MARGIE: I don't know what to do, Helena. I'm a
           week late with my period.
HELENA: Uh-oh. Sounds like you may be
           pregnant, huh?
MARGIE: Gee, I hope not.
HELENA: You and Bob have been using
           protection, right?
MARGIE: Yes, I use the sponge.
HELENA: Really?
MARGIE: Yes. I don't know if it worked right,
           though.
HELENA: Well, how did you put it in?
MARGIE: I just stuck it in after we had sex.
HELENA: Oh, no! No wonder! You never took the
           time to read the directions!
MARGIE: What?
HELENA: Well, if you had read the directions,
           you would have known that you put
           the sponge in BEFORE SEX. And you
           would have known that you wet it first.
           Otherwise, it does not work.

The Sponge

Effectiveness:	HIGH
Health Safety:	Very Good
How It Works:	Like a diaphragm, it covers the cervix. It absorbs the sperm.
Side Effects:	None
Side Benefits:	May help reduce the risks of some STDs
OTHER FACTS:	The sponge cannot be left in for more than 30 hours at a time. Sponges should not be reused.

Like condoms, sponges are widely available in drugstores. They are usually found with feminine hygiene products. The most popular brand is called the "Today Sponge." Each sponge costs about $1.50 and one size fits all.

How the Sponge Works

The sponge works like a diaphragm does. It is inserted into the vagina and covers the cervix. There it traps and absorbs all the sperm. The spermicide inside each sponge kills the sperm.

How to Use the Sponge

The sponge must be wetted before it is inserted. This makes the spermicide work. The sponge may foam a little when it is wet. This is only the spermicide working.

Before inserting, hold the sponge with its string hanging down. The string will help when you want to remove the sponge. Pinch the edges of the sponge together and spread the lips of the vagina. Slide the sponge up as far as it will go. It should rest up against the pubic bone and cover the cervix. Just like a diaphragm.

The sponge can be inserted up to a day before intercourse. It should be left in for six to eight hours after intercourse. In all, the sponge should not be left in for more than 30 hours. If you have sex more than once during that time, extra spermicide should be added to the sponge with an applicator. Do not take the sponge out to do this.

The sponge can be removed by reaching into the vagina and taking hold of the string. The sponge should slide out easily. Sometimes the sponge turns around during sex. This may cause the string to move around too. With a little effort, the string can be found.

Safety, Pluses and Minuses

The sponge is almost as effective as the condom or diaphragm. It has no common side effects or risks with use.

You cannot get a diaphragm without a prescription. The sponge can be bought without a prescription. But it can be more difficult to remove than a diaphragm.

Chapter 10

Spermicides

Spermicides are chemicals that trap sperm and kill it. Spermicides come in four basic types: Vaginal suppositories (tablets that are inserted into the vagina), foam, jelly, and cream. They are all available without a prescription. They are all fairly cheap to use. Spermicides are usually used along with condoms or diaphragms for extra effectiveness. They can be used alone, but they are not as effective that way.

VAGINAL SUPPOSITORIES are removed from the wrapper and inserted into the vagina. Most suppositories need time to dissolve in the vagina before sex. Most tablets need at least 30 minutes to dissolve properly.

	Spermicides
Effectiveness:	HIGH WITH OTHER PRODUCTS MEDIUM ALONE
Health Safety:	Good
How It Works:	Inserted before sex, it traps sperm
Side Effects:	None
Side Benefits:	None
OTHER FACTS:	Spermicides must be used in advance to let them dissolve. They should be used before each individual instance of sex.

JELLIES AND CREAMS are placed into the vagina with a special applicator. The applicator is usually included in the package. The applicator is filled with the jelly or cream, then put gently into the vagina. Each time you have sex, you must use a separate dose of cream or jelly beforehand.

FOAMS are also placed into the vagina with an applicator. Foams usually come in containers that must be shaken well before use. Foam gives protection at once. But it only lasts for thirty minutes. So foam should be put in just before sex.

With foam, you should not douche for at least six hours after sex.

The Effectiveness of Spermicides

Spermicides work much less well than condoms, diaphragms, or sponges. They need to be used each time before sex. And they need to be used properly. Be sure to use enough so that it will be effective. And they all must always be used BEFORE sex.

The Added Benefits of Spermicides

Beside being a contraceptive, spermicides also lubricate (oil). Lubrication often makes sex more comfortable and enjoyable. Spermicides may also protect against risks of giving your partner some STDs. Some scientists believe that they may kill some of the germs that cause some STDs.

Condoms and Spermicides Together: The Best on Three Counts

Many people use condoms with spermicides. That means the man wears a condom and the woman puts spermicide into her vagina. This is an excellent idea for three reasons. First, it works as well as the pill for birth control. Second, it is the best known way to prevent STDs. Third, the man and the woman can both protect against pregnancy and sexually transmitted diseases.

Chapter 11

Special Issues: IUDs and Abortion

IUDs

IUDs are another method of birth control. An IUD (intra-uterine device) is a plastic coil that is inserted into the uterus. It prevents an egg from fastening in the wall of the uterus. This prevents pregnancy.

Most doctors feel that teens should not use IUDs. Teens can easily accidentally push out an IUD. Teens also often have STDs, and an IUD can make things worse if bacteria of an STD have entered the uterus.

Because IUDs are not a good choice for teens, we will not discuss them in detail here.

Abortion

Abortion means ending a pregnancy before full term. ABORTION IS NOT A METHOD OF CONTRACEPTION. It does not prevent pregnancy. This book's purpose is to help *prevent* pregnancy. Preventing pregnancy is using contraception.

Chapter 12

STDs and Contraception

Sexually transmitted diseases (STDs) are a very serious problem in the United States.

STDs are spread mostly by sexual contact. That means contact between two people with the penis, the vagina, the anus, or the mouth. STDs are bacteria, viruses, and microbes. They are all microscopic organisms that invade the body and cause disease. Most of these organisms are very fragile. They cannot live outside the body. That is why they cannot be spread by toilet seats, doorknobs, or handshakes. The organisms cannot penetrate skin that is sealed. They can only get into the body through breaks in the skin or mucous membranes. These membranes can be found in the mouth, vagina, penis, and anus.

Sometimes an STD infection can happen without the infected person knowing it. Some diseases can "hide" in the body before coming out. Others appear and then seem to "go away." But they do not. You just can't see them. And many STD can be dangerous if they are not treated. There are a few points to remember about STD

o A person can get more than one STD at a time.
o You can have an STD without knowing it.
o People often lie about their sexual past. Asking your partner if he/she has an STD will not always get you an honest answer.
o Anyone can get an STD. Personality and cleanliness have nothing to do with it.
o The more often you have sex, the greater your risk. And the risk gets even higher with every new partner you have.

Contraceptives Can Help Reduce Risks of STDs
Some methods of contraception work quite well in reducing the risks of STDs.
Condom and Spermicide: The best safety known (other than no sex at all).
Condom Alone: Very good.
Spermicides: Fair but not sure. They can possibly kill some bacteria and microbes of certain STDs.
The Sponge and Diaphragm: Fair but not sure. The spermicides in both may help to reduce some risks.
The Pill: Very poor.

The following is a brief listing of the most common STDs and their symptoms. If you have any of these symptoms, or have had sex with someone who does, see a doctor right away.

AIDS (virus): Not common among teens who do not use intravenous drugs (drugs that are shot into the body with a needle). The disease cannot be cured and almost always causes death.

Herpes (virus): Not a major health threat. Does not do very serious damage to the body. Causes periodic sores and rashes on the genitals, anus, or mouth that can be painful. Herpes cannot be cured. The virus will stay in the body for life. But it can be treated to reduce symptoms.

Syphilis (bacteria): Can be cured with drugs. Can kill if not cured. Can "hide in the body" (be present without symptoms). Causes sores on genitals, mouth, and anus.

Gonorrhea (bacteria): Very common STD with teens. Can cause serious health threats, including sterility. Symptoms are pain and burning during urination and discharge from the vagina or penis.

Genital Warts (virus): Though not well known, genital warts are the most common STD in the United States. If you don't treat warts they can cause serious health problems.

Chlamydia (bacteria): Very like gonorrhea. It has similar symptoms and effects if not treated. Can cause sterility if not treated. Can be treated with drugs.

Chapter 13

Conclusion

Now you have learned about most of the methods of birth control you can use. You have seen how each one works. You have seen the good points and the bad points of each method. Hopefully, you at least know that ANY method is better than no method.

Many people know very little about contraception. Sometimes sex is too embarrassing for people to talk about. Many people don't ask questions. And most people think certain things about birth control that are not true. It's too bad that those people often get pregnant when they do not want to.

The only way to protect your health and happiness is to know about your body. Learning about sex and STDs is a very important part of that knowledge. With that information you can plan the methods of birth control that are best for you.

Many different birth control methods have been talked about in this book. We hope you can see that many of them are quite easy to use. And maybe you have decided on one or two methods to try. Most important, you should see that "safer sex" and healthy sex involve responsibility. And responsibility includes both the man and the woman when it comes to sex.

Maybe these chapters have helped you to think about sex or birth control in a different way. And maybe there are still some things that are not clear to you. If there are, you should go back and read it again. Try your best to understand. If you still don't understand, don't be afraid to ask someone. Talk to your doctor, or a school nurse. Talk to a teacher or guidance counselor. Visit a clinic. You'll soon see that finding out the truth is always much better than making mistakes.

Glossary—*Explaining New Words*

abortion   The ending of a pregnancy.
abstinence   Not having sex.
adolescence   Teen years.
AIDS   Acquired Immune Deficiency Syndrome, a fatal STD.
anatomy   Make up of the body.
anxieties   Uncomfortable feelings.

cervical cap   Contraceptive that fits over the cervix, like a diaphragm but smaller.

cervix   Opening of uterus.

chlamydia   Sexually transmitted bacteria, similar to gonorrhea.

clitoris   "Bump" near vagina that becomes excited to orgasm during sex.

condom   Contraceptive, rubber casing that fits over the erect penis.

consequences   Results of an action.

contraceptive   Birth control device.

diaphragm   Contraceptive, inserted into vagina and fits over the cervix.

douche   To wash or rinse out the vagina with a liquid.

ejaculate   For men, orgasm, to "come."

embryo   First stage of development, before fetus.

estrogen   Female hormone.

fallopian tubes   Connect the uterus to the ovaries.

fertilize   To create life, to begin pregnancy.

fertility   Ability to reproduce, create offspring.

fetus   Developing baby.

genital warts   Common sexually transmitted virus.

gonorrhea   Sexually transmitted bacteria.

gynecologist   Doctor who specializes in the female body.

herpes   An incurable sexually transmitted virus.

hymen   Skin inside vagina, usually broken with first sexual experience.

ignorance   Lack of knowledge.

IUD   Contraceptive, plastic device inserted into uterus.

labia   Lips of the vagina.

masturbation   Sexual self-stimulation.

menarche   A woman's first menstrual period.

menopause   When a woman stops menstruating (later in life).

menstrual cycle   Female monthly bleeding, also "period."

obstetrician   A doctor who specializes in caring for pregnant women.

orgasm   Male ejaculation, female stimulation of the clitoris, both also known as "coming."

ovaries   Produce eggs in the female.

ovulation   When egg is released from ovary into fallopian tube.

pap test   Test to detect cervical cancer and STDs.

penis   Male sexual organ.

premature   Too early.

puberty   Beginning of sexual, hormonal changes in the body.

pubic hair   Hair covering or surrounding the genitals.

rhythm method (of birth control)   Not having sex during most fertile times of the month.

sperm   Male fertilizing organism.

spermicide   Contraceptives, jellies or creams that are used with other birth control devices and that kill sperm.

status   Being admired by others.
STDs   Sexually transmitted diseases.
syphilis   Sexually transmitted bacteria.
testicles   Male sperm producers, "balls."
the pill   Contraceptive, taken orally. One of the most effective and popular forms of birth control.
the sponge   Contraceptive. Holds contraceptive jelly and foam and absorbs sperm inside the vagina.
uterus   Womb, where fetus grows and is nourished.
womb   See "uterus."

Where To Get Help

Birth Control Institute
1242 W. Lincoln Ave., Suite 7–10
Anaheim, CA 92805
Telephone: (714) 956-4630

Institute for Family Research and Education
Slocum Hall, Room 110
Syracuse, NY 13210
Telephone: (315) 423-4584

Planned Parenthood Federation of America, Educational Resources
810 Seventh Ave.
New York, NY 10019
Telephone: (212) 541-7800

Human Life and Natural Family Planning Foundation
5609 Broadmoor Street
Alexandria, VA 2231
Telephone: (703) 836-3377

For Further Reading

Belcastro, Philip A. *The Birth Control Book*, New York: Jones & Bartlett, 1986. A guide to all popular methods of birth control, each described in detail.

Benson, Michael D. *Coping with Birth Control*, New York: Rosen Publishing, 1988. Thorough coverage of biology, and birth control methods. It also discusses problems of teen sex. With a question & answer section, illustrations.

Planned Parenthood. *A Guide to Birth Control: Seven Accepted Methods of Contraception*, New York: Planned Parenthood Foundation, 1985. A medically oriented guide to the proper usage of seven major birth control methods with illustrations and instructions.

Westheimer, Ruth and Kravetz, Nathan. *First Love: A Young People's Guide to Sexual Information*, New York: Warner Books, 1985. A friendly discussion of teenage sexual behavior, with stories and personalized accounts.

White, Elizabeth K. *Birth Control and You*, New York: Budlong, 1987. Expores the questions of how one can decide on which birth control methods are best for each individual.

Index

About the Author

Dr. Mucciolo is an obstetrician/gynecologist at the New York University Medical Center. He also has a private practice in Manhattan and has cared for many teenagers and adolescents during his career.

About the Editor

Evan Stark is a well-known sociologist, educator, and therapist as well as a popular lecturer on women's and children's health issues. Dr. Stark was the Henry Rutgers Fellow at Rutgers University, an associate at the Institution for Social and Policy Studies at Yale University, and a Fulbright Fellow at the University of Essex. He is the author of many publications in the field of family relations and is the father of four children.

Acknowledgments and Photo Credits
Photographs by Stuart Rabinowitz; p. 8, 11, 19, Sonja Kalter

Design/Production: Blackbirch Graphics, Inc.
Cover Photograph: Stuart Rabinowitz